Weather Wise

Rain

Helen Cox Cannons

Heinemann LIBRARY

Chicago, Illinois

Edited by Siân Smith and John-Paul Wilkins
Designed by Philippa Jenkins and Peggie Carley
Picture research by Ruth Blair
Production by Victoria Fitzgerald
Originated by Capstone Global Library Ltd
Printed and bound in China by Leo Paper Group

18 17 16 15 14
10 9 8 7 6 5 4 3 2 1

Library of Congress Cataloging in Publication Data
Cataloging-in-publication information is on file with the Library of Congress.
ISBN 978-1-4846-0545-5 (hardcover)
ISBN 978-1-4846-0555-4 (paperback)
ISBN 978-1-4846-0570-7 (eBook PDF)

Photo Credits
Corbis: Steve Cole/Anyone/amanaimages, cover; Dreamstime: Egonzitter, 22, Hassanmohiudin, 4, Qwasyx, 18; iStockphoto: aimintang, 14, 23 (bottom), IsaacLKoval, 6, 23 (top), Krakozawr, 5, oriba, 20; Shutterstock: Balazs Kovacs, 21, Charlie Edward, 11, 23 (second from bottom), Dirk Ott, 10, Huansheng Xu, 7, leospek, 9, Matej Hudovernik, 8, 23 (middle), Viorel Sima, 15; SuperStock: Lisette Le Bon, 19

We would like to thank John Horel for his invaluable help in the preparation of this book.

Every effort has been made to contact copyright holders of material reproduced in this book. Any omissions will be rectified in subsequent printings if notice is given to the publisher.

Contents

What Is Rain?

Rain is water that falls from clouds.

Rain feels wet on your skin.

Types of Rain

When rain falls, it can be light rain.
This is sometimes called **drizzle**.

When rain falls, it can be heavy rain.

This is sometimes called a downpour.

In some places, it does not rain for a long time. There is not enough water.

This is called a **drought**.

In some places, it rains for a long time. There is too much water.

This is called a **flood**.

How Does Rain Form?

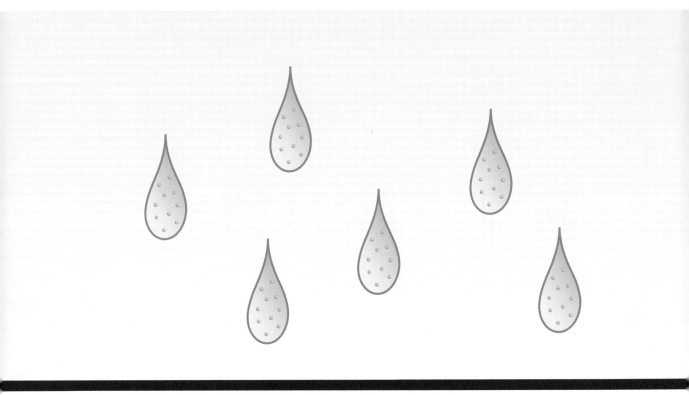

One raindrop is made from tiny drops of water. Each tiny drop is called a **droplet**.

When the Sun warms water, some of the water becomes a gas. This gas is called **vapor**.

vapor

Vapor comes from oceans, rivers, and lakes. Vapor even comes from puddles.

Vapor also comes from plants and animals. We usually cannot see this vapor.

The vapor rises into the air. Then it cools down and turns into droplets. The droplets make clouds.

The droplets join together and form raindrops. When the raindrops get too heavy, they fall to the ground.

What Do You Wear in Rainy Weather?

When it rains, you could wear a raincoat.

When it rains, you could also use an umbrella.

How Does Rain Help Us?

Rain brings water back down to Earth. It keeps the oceans filled.

Rain helps plants grow.

Did You Know?

Forests that have a lot of rain are called rain forests.

Picture Glossary

 **drizzle** light rain

 **droplet** tiny drop of water

 **drought** long period without rainfall

 **flood** large amount of water that spreads over dry land

 **vapor** gas created by heating water

23

Index

Notes for Parents and Teachers

Before Reading
Assess background knowledge. Ask: What is rain? How does rain form? How does rain help us?

After Reading
Recall and reflection: Ask children if their ideas about rain at the beginning were correct. What new facts about rain did they learn?

Sentence knowledge: Ask children to look at page 13. How many sentences are on the page? Have them point to the beginning and end of one sentence.

Word recognition: Have children point at the word *some* on page 8 and 10. Can they think of another word that means about the same as *some*?